# Naiad Blood

*poems by*

# Sarah C. Beckmann

*Finishing Line Press*
Georgetown, Kentucky

# Naiad Blood

Sarah C. Beckmann is a current MFA candidate at Emerson College (Boston, MA). As an undergraduate, Sarah was chosen as the Student Poet representing Trinity College (CT) in the 2018 Connecticut Poetry Circuit. She was one of five poets selected from a variety of nominees, and toured the state with fellow winners from Yale University, Quinnipiac University, Wesleyan University, and Middlesex Community College. During her four years at Trinity, she was a member of the women's crew team—an experience that has heavily influenced her writing.

She lives in Boston, where she is a member of Union Boat Club on the Charles River and has the opportunity to continue rowing; she works at the MIT Media Lab in Cambridge. She frequently travels back and forth between Boston and her childhood home in Manchester-by-the-Sea, MA, as well as the town of Southold on the North Fork of Long Island, NY, where her grandfather lives.

Her work has been published previously by the Academy of American Poets and the *Under Review*.

## ACKNOWLEDGMENTS

"Duende" (originally titled "Duende in Rowing") is previously published on
the Academy of American Poets website.
"homage to my legs" is previously published online by the *Under Review*.

I am especially grateful for the support and critiques of my classmates,
particularly from Livia Meneghin and Audrey Dubois, as well as the
thoughtful guidance and sharp edits from our professor Daniel Tobin. I'm
forever appreciative of my best friend and fellow poet Bhumika Choudhary,
who I love dearly and is always ready to read my work. Credit is also due
to my wonderful undergraduate advisor Clare Rossini, who helped me
develop a number of poems in this collection while I was working on my
thesis. And for my main creative inspiration, I can't be thankful enough to my
former teammates and coaches on the women's crew team at Trinity College,
CT. Rowing has changed my life, and thank you for welcoming me into
this amazing and hard-working family. To my personal family and friends,
including most notably Linda Crosby and her family: thank you for coming
to my readings, and for never ceasing to believe in me.

Publisher: Leah Huete de Maines
Editor: Christen Kincaid
Cover Art: Renee Jones
Author Photo: Courtney Nicole Photography
            (https://courtneynicolephotography.squarespace.com)
Cover Design: Elizabeth Maines McCleavy


Order online: www.finishinglinepress.com
            also available on amazon.com

Author inquiries and mail orders:
Finishing Line Press
PO Box 1626
Georgetown, Kentucky 40324
USA

*"Yes, as every one knows, meditation and water are wedded for ever."*
—Herman Melville, *Moby-Dick*

*"And if you were a proper lady, you didn't row at all."*
—Daniel J. Boyne, *The Red Rose Crew*

# Table of Contents

**peconic summers**

ok yes i'm in love with
jingle shells and jelly fish

but i'm talking about the
see-through ones that aren't
pink and don't sting the ones
that drag shadows like dark
freckles in the shallows the ones
that make you shudder when you
touch their gooey ghosts

i'm talking about sea robins
blowfish sand sharks and porgies
skates and horseshoe crabs things
you catch off your grandfather's
boat before you jump off and
paddle to the beach where mom sits
in a chair we've had since the 60s

i'm talking about a road south
of the harbor where we swim
across a channel our annual
migration to the white point
of land that juts out like a chin
into caribbean blue water

i'm talking about a farmhouse
a rope swing with a tractor tire
wooden adirondack chairs and gas
lanterns on tables with sunflowers
sweet corn on the cob and barefoot
children running beneath the stars

i'm talking about hammocks
rocking chairs and chalk drawings
on the driveway a garage full of
bicycles a blue and white house
a porch with a view—it's all about

laughter floating through an open
window on a summer firefly night
up into the black like
chinese lanterns        fading

## A Life through Boats, I

*To the Mary Ellen, Cape Henlopen, John H., and Susan Anne*

Your jaw opens and gives us entry
to your steel bowels. Our car nestles
between your ribs, tight, sometimes
a real squeeze—but you never fail
to consume us all, and our wheels.

You let out a long,
reverberating honk, and we watch
as, on both sides, land slowly slides away.
Beneath our feet, the deep vibration of your
well-conditioned heart, the new constant.

You pump us into sea,
past Plum Island, into the Gut, around
the Orient Point Lighthouse—*Grammy's
Lighthouse*, black, white,
and regal as a coffee pot.

You have carried me back and forth
between two homes since my body
was new, your pulse as familiar
as my mother's heartbeat,
your buoyant rocking
safe as her womb.

## A Life through Boats, II

*To the Dyer Dhows, Optis, 420s, and Rhodes 19s*

Hat, sunscreen, bathing suit, life jacket,
whistle, and booties: with these, I learned
to tie eight knots, square knots. To rig
boats, fold and roll sails on the dock.
To sky a line—and how

to capsize, slipping into water
on a cold, cloudy day; lying, drenched,
on your exposed center board, levering
you upright with my weight,
terrified.

I was that girl who hugged your mast,
eyes closed, crying, fearing
the moment when you tipped too far
and we all went falling over
again—

that girl who stood in your stern,
tiller in one hand, mainsheet in the other,
tacking, jibing, dancing with the boom,
as the wind whipped and split the ends
of my hair, long, loose, wild.

As my body grew, I sailed, and knew
the power of air.

**Women and Water**


Women and water do not mix.
For a female onboard is bad luck at sea;
Blood blooms in those wayward depths.

Men, in ancient myths,
Wrecked ships at sirens' song, deadly sweet.
Women and water do not mix.

But, bright against Mother Nyx,
The moon, too, tugs our tides, our bodies;
Blood blooms in those wayward depths.

We live this truth, red as bricks,
Crimson as Ophelia's flooded veins.
Women and water do not mix.

But, at the sight of a woman's breasts,
Rough waters calm; naked figureheads keep
Blood from blooming in those wayward depths.

       Grace O'Malley, at her father's refusal, axed
       Her hair to ride a ship—and became a sea queen.
       Ha! Women and water do not mix!

Strong as an oath on the River Styx,
As superstition is, who could really believe
Women and water do not mix, that
Blood blooms in those wayward depths?

## Oracle

*Inspired by Gwendolyn Brooks's* Annie Allen

Young girl passes, bold as a butcher's blade,
doesn't know her sharpness; a baroness blade.
Maiden, laden with old dreams of romance,
studies the seasons—and eyes a man's blade.

Dimples, dabs powder, rims her lips with pink—
ears prick to low thrum, advancing drums, blades.
She sighs. Her hair won't grow past the shoulder…
can curls dare swirl beneath regretless blade?—

She walks the riverbank…water whispers
of drums, beginnings—*drop fairy love's blade,*
say the waves. *Wield woman's weapon,* an oar
in your hard hands, not someone else's blade—

*Princess, daughter of Mars,* heed the call: trade
skirts and diadem—for unisuit, vortex blade.

## Phantom Pains

In dreams, I touch my hair,
chestnut locks, longer
than they ever were in reality.

I play with them, pull them up
in a ponytail, wag my head
and revel
in the soft and swaying.

Sensations
I can almost remember, of something
no longer there. I wake up forgetting.

Did Medusa weep
when her hair began to hiss?
What of Rapunzel and Sif,
both with their golden tresses
severed?

Some say when a woman
cuts her curls, she loses more
than her hair.

> The Navajo divines a connection between
> hair and memory; the longer the strands,
> the longer the past lives.
>> I must seem absent-minded.

> In Chinese tradition, cropped hair means
> banishment from the family, rejection.
>> I must be homeless.

> Hindu women only scissor their hair
> when widowed, their womanhood so closely tied
> to their husbands.
>> I must be a widow.

In wider belief, short-haired women
are not youthful, feminine.
                    I must not be beautiful.

But then I see Mulan—a flash of silver and straight,
black straw falling to the floor. I see her steal
her father's sword, disguised
to fight for China.

I see Joan of Arc in full armor, hair bobbed,
warring for France, and, later,
in a prison cell, awaiting her sentence,
before sainthood.

Some time has passed, and those phantom dreams
still pain me—but, more often now,
I stride from the dresser door leaving dark tufts
on the ground,
feeling so light I could almost
                                    laugh!

I know why,
after her first flight, Amelia Earhart

chopped her hair.

# How to Gain Muscle

You sweat,
everyday. You

squat with a bar on your shoulders,
a concrete-filled paint can on each side.

You wake up early
and lie on a bench, press
a bar with two and a half pounds,
five pounds, ten pounds—
fifteen, then twenty on each side—

You trap bar deadlift
more than your body weight—
*one* time, breathe, *two* times—
breathe—

> You ignore your screaming hands
> as the weight of eight other bodies
> crushes the calluses on your skin, as you
> push an oar through water, propel
> the shell forward—one stroke after
> another—
>
> You lift that vessel out of water and
> over your head, arms locked,
> knees steady—the lone fisherman
> on the dock in shock, watching you—
>
> he watches you and your sisters,
> you strong, Amazon warriors—
>
> because women are not *supposed* to have muscle;
> women are not *supposed* to be strong—
>
> because not everyone can do
> what you do,
>
> everyday.

## A Life through Boats, III

*To the Ruffian, Spectacular Bid, Kraft, Unbowed, Alydar,*
*A4+, and Z4+*


I came to rowing
lanky, wide-eyed, the skin on my hands
soft. I was a girl raised by the sea, I thought
I knew the water.

I thought I was a woman. But she appeared
only after

I popped my first blister. After the calluses
on my palms turned yellow. After I couldn't see
my toes past my thighs, learned to lift weights,
boats. To win silver medals under blinding skies.

My bones as strong as the carbon fiber
that held me.

The woman I became first breathed
on a seat that barely spans the width of my hips,
sliding, unstable, an oar in my hand that seemed more
like a javelin. The rigger on my right side, wing-like,
my blade one feather out of many.

> I am a passenger, a single cog in your engine.
> But something greater within all of us
> feeds you; you ride on those
> inner winds, intangible, yet

> stronger than any machine.

## The Rower's Dichotomy

The mechanical dragon
crouches on the ground,
waiting for me
to climb on her back—taunting me
to dare.

She's an Ergometer,
of the Dynamic species, and her name
is Concept 2.

I settle into my saddle, grasp
the metallic reins, and at
the kick of my spurs her wheel
turns with a hiss and roar.

I stare into her
square face, into the mouth
that spits out numbers, into the eyes
that see nothing but glory
in pain.

She's the only dragon I know
that never flies.

                                      The onyx vessel
sits in slings,
waiting for us
to pick her up—smiling at us
in the sun.

She's a boat,
a carbon-fiber shell, and her name
is the *Unbowed*.

We lift her up, carry her
on our shoulders, and at
the call of our coxswain, we
place her in the water.

We admire her
cylindrical curves, the way water
wicks from her sides, and those
sliding seats oiled
with WD-40.

She's the only boat we know
that can fly.

I sit astride you in my
organic armor, my
body as my only weapon.

The distance is set. A sacrifice
made: as a woman,

I am already bleeding
before the war.

We sit inside you in our
matching uniforms, our
bodies in numbered order.

The distance is buoyed. Our backs
face the finish line: as women,

some of us are bleeding
before the battle.

You
breathe fire into me—I can feel it
blazing through my muscles—scorching
my every tendon—smoldering
slowly up my spine—you're
hurting me—I'm
*hurting me—*
*hot—*
*hot—*

                                        You
          send a thrill through our veins—we can feel it
              jumping in our muscles—bouncing
                 through every bone—beaming
              like a light from our spirits—you're
                    moving us—we're
                        *moving us—*
                           *bright—*
                           *bright—*

                    The distance ends.

I look
       up
            now   at
      your
animated   face
                 covered
            in
      numbers      and
                   I see—
        I see—
                 black

                                        We look
                                      up
                                   now    at
                                            the
                                   bright blue   sky—
                                        our
                                   breathing
                                   synchronized—we
                                        are
                                   one body—we
                                        are
                                   one mind—we
                                        are

                                   *us.*

## homage to my legs

*With thanks to Lucille Clifton*


these legs are long legs.
they need room to
stretch out in.
they can't cram into
small spaces. these legs
are strong legs;
they've never been broken.
these legs are pretty legs—

these legs move boats.

these legs know
the pain of two thousand meters.
they don't rush. they're
*smoooth* up the slide as if the tracks
were coated with butter.
they're patient. they wait
for the boat to come
to them. and they don't slam
the front end; they
land with the softness
of a butterfly's beating wings.

## Of Rowers and Racehorses

The first boat I ever rowed
was the *Ruffian*, black as her namesake
and bred for medaling. Big for a filly,
but well proportioned—the shoes

on her foot stretchers just my size,
as if I was born to race with her.
If Secretariat was king, *Ruffian*
was queen, Poseidon's thumbprint

shining, white as a star, on her forehead.
Undefeated and record setting
'til her last race—
until that day she died. As a rower,

I know her story. I know why
the racehorse runs.

***

Race day comes in early May. Names
line the jumbotron. Not Louisville, KY,
but Worcester, MA, where Gatorade,
grill smoke, parents sporting school attire

replace Mint Juleps, gambling, frilly hats—
and the dirt course swaps for lake water.
A bugle sounds. Coxswains rally
their rowers to the Post: at the command,

half-naked beasts heave *Ruffian* to waists,
to shoulders. Trot in the parade to the dock,
muscles rippling, shivering, ears
pricking to the call: "Riders Up!"

*Ruffian's* hull, cradled, kisses water.
Her rowers, descend. The coxswain mounts.

***

Officials corral us to our lane, hold us secure
within a buoyed cage. We wait, shaking. Soon
as the flag drops—when that bell rings—
"Attention: Go!"—*and down the stretch*

*they come*—hooves, oarlocks
crack like thunder, reverberate through
our bones; the coxswain hunches low
in the stern, crouches in her stirrups, hisses

sharp in our ears: *pick-it-up, pick-it-up,*
*on the legs, finding speed that's it*—eight oars
blink in the sun, beat like wings; our stride,
long—our cadence, demanding—if something

shatters—no matter; *we'll pull 'til our limbs break,*
'til we tear ourselves apart—running for more
than roses, we don't feel the reins—we only hear
our name. So when our time's up—bury us

by the racecourse,
nose pointed towards the finish line.

## Rigging

*From the Old English* wrigan *or* wrihan, *meaning "to clothe"*

Belly up, naked, I wait in slings,
hear their voices, feel their small hands
glide across my hull, probe
my sliding seats and foot stretchers.

They keep my wings in bags,

bolt them to my gunwales, lock them with washers,
plates, nuts—little fingers flutter, wrench them
tighter—too tight!—I feel

the heat of them, standing by my sides,
hear them curse when they forget a backstay,
hear them whisper, *righty tighty, lefty loosey.*

They wipe me down from stern deck
to bow ball; grease, wax, polish me
until I darkly sparkle with the promise
of speed. I'm heavier now,

but they know how to make
me move, lifting, grunting, walking me
to the water—running those long poles,
with their collars and sleeves,
through my feathers.

My nine hearts beat. I hear their thoughts, know
their dreams. My battle gear glistens; they always
dress me well—

they're the naked ones,
now.

## Duende

*It's a great art, is rowing. It's the finest art there is…And*
*when you're rowing well, why it's nearing perfection. And*
*when you near perfection, you're touching the Divine.*
—George Yeomans Pocock

We rowers have peculiar rituals. Like running
stairs indoors, inhaling
stale air and dust. Like sweating
in a tank room, all concrete walls and low ceiling,
mirrors and machines. Our suffering, artificial.

While we labor in these confines, we pray
in wintertime for blue skies, flat water.
For the sun.

We see in our minds that pavement path
that slopes, downward, to the river.
On one shoulder, our dark craft, we make
our morning pilgrimage: salute the waning moon,
the dawn.

> First light
> ricochets off water; the fragments
> shower our foggy faces. It's the thing
> that fully wakes us, makes
> the naiad blood in any girl
> sing.

On land, we abandon our bodies,
discard our separate shells in exchange
for a new vessel. The moment the last foot
leaves the dock, an unearthly link
completes itself.

> On water, our souls surrender,
> affix to that greater whole,
> that *oneness*—at the risk
> of becoming gods ourselves!—we
> glide through the waves, our togetherness

> the only thing that anchors us.

## If Persephone Rowed

Nothing says winter    like hands    aching for oars
creased    dry    cracked    itching to dip    a blade
and glide    across that glass.    The rower looks    out
from the bridge    into frosty    stillness    the river
a reptile    splintered in arctic    scales    dormant
in the cold. *Hibernation*    the word    an old man
chants    as he ergs    in a snowstorm.

A swan    stands on ice
neck bent    sees its reflection.
The cityscape    looms.

Spring is the sight of three shells—first of the season—
on the river; anyone who's rowed stops in their tracks
on the bridge, turns, watches. *Been waiting so long for
this moment*—the boat bay doors open—even if there's
still snow on the banks, bergs in the water—the call
to home—hard to ignore: it's the skin, knowing its
softness won't last—a tingling in the fingertips.

Purple palms—dead scabs,
drachmas. Blisters bloom, pink, red—
harden. Leather gloves.

## The Seat Race

Chains clank as the bay doors open. Coaches
load gas tanks in grocery carts, tow them down
the asphalt slope. A pack of tightly clad bodies
carries oars, launches on rollers, jostles and yips
up the hill. The sun rises, though not a hand

touches a boat. Every season, a time comes
when coaches talk *selection*. Hackles stand
at the word, ears flatten, tails tuck between
thighs, eyes watch each other. Walk-ons

get skittish. Juniors crack their joints, paw
the ground and snort. Recruits pick their teeth;
they know the drill. Some feel safe, others
fear for their seat—but at the apex of any team
lies a single rower, a predator in her prime:

five feet, ten inches of lean, toned ego. Hair
twitching like the tail of a Friesian horse, built
for speed and breaking records. Look directly
in her eye, and she snaps—jaw unhinged,
saliva streaming from her fangs—so hungry

she could eat a coxswain. Challenge her
for a spot in the top crew, and before the boats
hit the water—she spreads her arms, protracts
her claws, licks her lips. And grins.

# what rowers remember

ask a rower if they remember
a single race, and I guarantee
the things they'll remember

are the hotel breakfast food—yogurt,
plastic spoons, styrofoam plates, bananas,
frosted flakes—any fuel kept down,

the bus ride to the course,
the songs through their headphones,
walking to the trailer, running

in the maze of uniformed bodies,
boats, and asphalt, sweating
porta-potties, group meeting—

the boat resting, heavy;
bare shoulders, calves; sneakers, socks;
muscles tanned by the sun,

sculpted by months of training,
all leading to this moment:
sitting at the start, blade squared,

cars thundering on the bridge above
your coxswain, crooning—soon
as the flag falls—

as watching, fingers twitching,
other crews in the lanes beside you,
names being read—

*stay calm, don't balk*—the call!—
a blur—only movement
backwards, in time

movement, so fast it's blue, blurry—
a voice yelling, a foot tapping—
those unbearable moments, seconds—

the instant you know you're dying—
insides churning like volcanic lava—
frothing-at-the-mouth suffering—

and when it finally ends,
the sounds of heaving, breathing,
heart shuddering, fit to burst

in your mouth, the taste of blood,
mucus from your lungs, clogged—
laying back in your teammate's arms,

clutching your coxswain's hand,
the fire in your legs making you gag,
limp, wheezing, your legs

barely able to stand on the dock,
dry land, a foreign entity,
adrenaline sizzling,

still echoing through your bones—
the medal on your chest, great
but not as extraordinary

as *feeling*—
sitting on that lake,
on that sunny spring day—

the agony of seven minutes
to the finish line—forgotten
in wondering if, next race, you'll be ready

## Carpe diem

It's race day, and my strokes are numbered.
I watch shells—hundreds—go down the course.

Shells by the hundreds go down that course,
and my boat glides between the buoys.

I'm in the boat, between the buoys,
and I'm moving like a metronome,

rolling, steady as a metronome,
but my bones won't hold for much longer—

Lord knows, my bones won't hold much longer.
Memories beat like waves on the bow;

like waves, these words—they break on the bow,
and time slows as I row these waters.

*As we row, time slows our waters.*
On race day, I count my strokes. Numbered.

# Pilot

The rower behind me is a Pilot,
she flies planes for a living.
Before sunrise, the river's sleeping,
and I think of willows and gardens,
ducks landing like planes on the water.
The cityscape's lights make me dizzy.

In the dark, a whisper behind me, dizzy,
as, in a single, another Pilot
pulls up; Caryn Davies on the water,
deltoids popping. It's her living.
In the presence of greatness in gardens,
in this city, I don't waste time sleeping,

but I see homeless people sleeping
in the Common, the pigeons dizzy
with bread crumbs in the gardens.
I didn't know I could be a Pilot
until I started living
like a cormorant diving in the water.

The subway drips with water,
and sometimes I feel like sleeping,
but how could I? With so many living
bodies, coming and going in a dizzy
frenzy—how many can say they're a Pilot?
How many walk through these gardens,

take pause in these gardens,
see a blurry face in the water—
and feel like they're flying? Pilots
are always in danger of sleeping,
dreaming so much they feel dizzy—
not ones afraid of living.

Dogs crap on brick sidewalks. I'm living
with squirrels and frogs in the gardens.
The Hancock building makes me dizzy—
I'm so *thirsty* for the water—
blisters bubble my hands as I'm sleeping,
remind me that I am a Pilot

      living in Boston, a Pilot
      wandering in the gardens, found sleeping,
      dizzy from soaring. Desperate for water.

## On the Eve of Rower's Christmas

'Twas the night before Christmas, and all through the city
rowers lay tucked in their beds. Their presences, heavy,
pulsate like lights in the buildings. Soft-footed coxswains
watch over their broods; race plans and moves
dance in drowsy minds. Boats hum in slumber, oars thirst
for callused hands, and the river ripples, dark,
quiet. People from lands far and wide will journey
to these banks, to celebrate the birth of a god
named Charles. They send prayers for good weather,
for this coming dawn, in which they will rise immune
to the cold of late October. People will gather
on the bridges, greeting teammates of years past
as if no time lay between them, their voices ringing
like bells above the ships that propel beneath them.
The entrancing magic of an oar—as it cuts—
through water—brings them home, again and again,
on this day; the white crest of backsplash, a gift,
a reminder of what it is to be young and old and strong.

## Aubade for the River

*Leave off your bending to the oar, and glide*
*Past innocence, beyond these aging bricks,*
*To where the Charles flows in to join the Styx.*
                    —Adrienne Rich, "A Walk By the Charles"


I come to you in early morning. I walk the footbridge
over Storrow Drive, and you call to me—
gouge your hook into my spine; I can never resist
your gravity. Through a boat, I touch your waters

and welcome the rising sun, revel in the flames
glinting off you, illuminating bodies bent mid-stroke,
single-file shadows in stark relief against the ribs
of bridges. The searing images engrave my mind

as well as the concrete, like glyphs of ancient caves.
Yet I find myself in deeper danger, as I glance
over the gunwale, and see your gentle eyes reflect
back at me. Young and enamored, call me vain—

know when winter comes, I'll lie next to you, rest
an arm on your still, icy plane, hips pressed close
to your banks. I'll wait for spring to wake you,
for our love is much older than us. I want

to stroke your purling face in an endless echo,
row to where the seasons halt, and your touch
makes us invulnerable as the dawn.

## Pindar Vineyards

*Let these deep draughts of enchanted wine*
*Lift me in soarings high and far*
      —Pindar (522-443 B.C.)


From the Main Road, my eyes track grape trellises,
hang on each post, glimpse a column of earth
before catching on the next stake. Farm stands
on the roadside, rickety, run down, sell fresh produce:
corn ears, sugar donuts, honey sticks. The juice
of a Wickham's peach trickles down my chin. I think
of Briermere pie as I pass by fields so flat and green…
I picture myself running on them, past helixes of irrigation

to the old water pump behind the farmhouse. The time
of year when my skin, dark as the soles of my bare feet,
is restless as the guinea hens; two escape to the cab
of the yellow pickup. The time for tractor rides, as the light,
half-baked, waxes sherbert at sunset. We take photos
of our shadows, posing on the gray barn walls,

thinking summer will never end. I dream of being married
to these fields. No matter where I go, what I do,
I return to my godfather's land, where we dance and sing
the *epinikion*, and lift wine in crystal chalices.

## Coronarowing

When it comes to boat-moving, I know
a thing or two. Boat feel is a sixth sense.
Balance, rhythm, and timing; the coxswain's
voice soon becomes your conscience.

A thing or two: you feel the boat best
in stroke seat of an eight. Nine bodies,
voices, soon become your conscience;
shoes on the dock, the only trace of us.

Put me in stroke seat of an eight, my body's
happy place; my one-mind home. We leave
our shoes on the dock, our only trace—
but take big boats away. What are you now?

Not so happy, anymore. Home is empty,
and you're flipping singles in the Charles.
What's a girl to do, when big boats are gone?
Land legs grown too fond; small, fragile, bruised.

You're flipping singles in the Charles,
because you don't know how to read wind.
Your sea legs are lost, the bruises fade,
but the memories and voices do not.

You don't know how to read wind,
and small boats get scary in big water.
No memories, voices to guide you along—
the river is long, and the basin's deep.

Big water gets scary when you're all alone.
Balance, rhythm—coxswain—*where are you!*
The river is long, the basin's deep—and when
it comes to boat-moving, I thought I knew.

## Horizon Bound

You are 60 feet long and
220 pounds.

But I like to keep you on one shoulder.

I like to
keep you above the ground, as high
as my body can manage, because you
are my keeper.

I'm with you when the sun rises,
when the river steams with mist;
we sit in the cold tendrils, the wisps
shot through by the half-open eyelid
of morning.

I'm with you after sunset,
when orange rims the trees
like embers, when the water swirls
like ink,
like oil—
almost as black as you.

And when I put you down to rest
in our house, your weight
never truly leaves
my shoulder.

When I sleep I think of you. I dream
of what we do. I dream of you
holding me and my sisters, as we
push you toward the sky, eight oars pulling
higher, higher into flight as the waves
suck and slip at your hull—try
not to let you
go—

I dream of us dancing together,
together on the water, always

horizon bound.

CPSIA information can be obtained
at www.ICGtesting.com
Printed in the USA
LVHW052337110921
697589LV00002B/189